MW00379299

The Modern Day Virtuous Woman

12 Qualities of a Woman Connected to the Divine Source

WENDY WRAY

1

All the stories related to this book are true, but most of the names have been changed or omitted to protect the privacy of the people mentioned.

The Modern Day Virtuous Woman:
12 Qualities of a Woman Connected to the Divine Source
Copyright © 2017 by Wendy Wray
ISBN: 978-0-9992664-0-3

Printed in the United States of America.

AUTHOR'S BIO

WENDY WRAY is an international speaker, teacher, leader, spiritual counselor and certified life coach. Wendy challenges women to have standards of excellence in every area of their lives by helping them to realize that they can do all things through Christ who strengthens them. Through her international travel, Wendy has discovered that women all across the globe have a desire to be intimately connected to God and grow in their spiritual walk. Wendy has a master's degree in education, and she has also completed her doctorate in marital and family therapy at Loma Linda University. Wendy's mission in life is to help women to have a transformational experience by empowering them to trust God in every area of their lives and walk by faith, not by sight.

TABLE OF CONTENTS

ACKNOWLEDGMENTS

I would like to first and foremost thank the Lord my God for being so patient with me, giving me the vision and granting me the wisdom to write this book. I don't know what I would do without such heavenly counsel. I would like to acknowledge my mom, whom I love dearly, for always believing in me and being my number one cheerleader. Her support means the world to me. I would also like to thank my father, who now rests in peace, for leaving a legacy through his great counsel; his words of wisdom are engraved in my heart, and I will never forget them. I appreciate my siblings: Lavern, Anton, Charmain, and Dionne and my in-laws—Colin, Joan, and Roman for playing such an indispensable role in my life—spiritually, socially, and emotionally. Thanks for all the late-night talks, words of counsel, listening ears, and laughs. I thank God every day for the family He gave me; I would not be who I am today without them. I am thankful for my extended family for being a regular part of our family bi-weekly prayer line for over four years. Our prayer group has helped to increase my faith, and I have experienced the miraculous power of prayer as a family. I also want to thank Pastor Michael Bernard for showing me how to lead others in love by being a caring shepherd to his flock whether near or far. Your demonstration of unconditional love has touched me and changed my life forever.

I want to thank my Metropolitan church family in Maryland and my Mt. Rubidoux church family in California for their continued prayers and support. I want to give special thanks to my sisters in Christ who have been a part of my prayer groups over the years. Thank you for your support and prayers. To my dear childhood and long-time friends from college, ladies, you know who you are; thank you for hanging in there no matter what. I love you girls! Thank you all for your encouragement and for always believing that it was just a matter of time before I published a book, and to everyone else who believed that this book would be the first of many to come.

Finally, I want to pay special tribute to those who were selected to read and provide input for my first draft. Thank you for taking the time to go through it thoroughly and for offering honest feedback. This book would not be what it is without all of you.

I want to say special thanks to my first editor, Grace. Grace, I thank God for your editing touch in helping me to pursue my first draft. Here we are several years later, and my book is now in its final draft and print.

Thank you ALL from the bottom of my heart. May the Lord pour out such blessings on you all that you will not have enough room to receive them!

INTRODUCTION

Have you ever heard it said that perception is reality? If you think about it, you will realize that there is truth to that theory. When you believe that something is true, you no longer embrace alternative interpretations; your perception of the situation becomes the accepted reality. This can affect you in positive or negative ways.

Take for example, the story of a married couple that had invited another couple into their home to spend a few days with them. Shortly after the visiting couple left, a female undergarment was found in the dryer. The wife immediately accused her husband of having an affair. The husband declared truthfully that he did not know where the underwear came from and fervently denied that he was having an affair. But his wife had already decided that he was guilty, and she allowed her perception to become her reality. The couple argued over this matter so much that they were considering divorce. Several weeks later, the wife of the couple who had visited them earlier called and sheepishly announced that she had lost her favorite underwear and wanted to know if they had seen it. After hearing the description of the garment, the wife immediately realized her perception had been wrong and that her husband was indeed telling the truth. Of course, she apologized to her husband for falsely accusing him and not believing his explanations. But it was a misunderstanding that almost cost them their marriage.

Ladies, I shared this story because I want to emphasize the crucial role your perception plays in your life. Whether you see things negatively or positively, your perception enormously impacts your life. So, as we take this journey together to learn "The 12 Qualities of a Woman Connected to the Divine Source," I ask you to keep these themes close to your heart. Reflect on them daily until they become a part of you. If a behavior becomes a habit with repetition, then believe in faith that you have the God-given ability to develop new habits and eliminate old destructive habits. Start practicing these qualities daily for as long as it takes to become a part of you. When you ask God to answer a prayer, it doesn't have to be a long, drawn out eloquent prayer. You simply have to pray in faith and be obedient to the voice of the Lord. As you commune with God throughout the day, remember to sing praises to His Holy name. Believe that God has granted you favor in whatever the situation is and claim the victory despite the odds.

You must claim it, but first, you must believe it in your heart, even if what you see does not seem to measure up to what you are asking of God. Remember, your perception is your reality. Are you able to trust God completely?

The key is asking and expecting blessings to come, regardless of your present circumstance. Each day, you will grow stronger in the Lord as we work together, pray together, testify together and put God first in our lives. We must learn to believe that perfect love cast out all fear (1 John 4:18). We must declare that negative thoughts and doubts have no place in our lives and believe that God has great things in store for His children. Thank you all for joining me on this journey as you read my first book. I hope that it is a journey that will bless your life as it has and continues to bless mine each time I read and apply these principles.

A WOMAN OF FAITH

B ut let him ask in faith, with no doubting, for he who doubts is like a wave of the sea driven and tossed by the wind. For let not that man suppose that he will receive anything from the Lord; he is a double-minded man, unstable in all his ways (James 1:6-8, NKJV).

How many times have we let the very same thoughts that work for us, work against us? We start off excited, expecting the best and a few obstacles get in the way or we experience an unexpected delay and we start to waver, doubt or ask what if....maybe this isn't for me after all. Maybe this isn't God's plan for my life. The Lord has already confirmed it countless times in so many different ways, but yet still, we question Him in the midst of the storm. The very same thoughts that once worked for us are now working against us. Many people do not understand what faith really is and have not begun to practice living their lives by faith. If we are always waiting to see the results, then we are not walking by faith, because "faith is the substance of things hoped for, the evidence of things not seen" (Hebrews 11:1). To truly walk in faith is to believe in the unexpected; to envision the unimaginable; to see what is not yet visible; to expect the impossible to become possible.

A BIBLICAL WOMAN OF FAITH

One of the best stories of faith in the Bible is the woman with the issue of blood for 12 years. When she heard Jesus was coming, she did not fret over a myriad of questions — worrying about what other people would think or say, wondering if He could heal her. No, she believed in faith that if she could just reach through the crowd and touch the hem of His garment, she would be made whole. Indeed, Jesus said, "because of your faith, you are made whole" (Matthew 9:21-22). This woman believed without a shadow of a doubt that she would be healed and eventually she received the desires of her heart.

MODERN DAY WOMEN OF FAITH

When I think of a testimony that required great faith, where the Lord showed up and showed out, the one that touches my heart most is a nurse who attends my church in Maryland. She was working at the hospital as she did every day when suddenly she heard a loud crash in a nearby room. She rushed to investigate and found that a patient had fallen to the floor and was screaming. She immediately ran toward him and reached out to lift him up. However, his body weight was more than twice her own, and her efforts to help him up left her with a ruptured disc in her back. She was confined to bed rest and had been convalescing for several months when three members of our Women's Ministries Group went to her home to visit and pray with her. Our prayers were of faith and one accord; there was no doubt in our minds that by the grace of God she could be healed. Each member of the group prayed, including the injured woman, who confessed her sins and poured out her heart to our Heavenly Father. One member rubbed her aching body with oil as we prayed for healing. Afterward, the woman who had lain on bed rest for months rose to her feet with tears of joy; her faithful God had healed her. She then knelt to thank God for her healing. Her daughter entered the room in disbelief, and her husband came home from work, also in disbelief. This was truly a testimony of faith. Everyone agreed, petitioning God with unwavering faith, confessing and asking for forgiveness of past sins, and believing that she could be healed despite her circumstances. Jehovah Rapha heals!

HOW DO I BECOME A WOMAN OF FAITH?

As we develop faith, we begin to trust God more. Increased faith is developed over time. Every time you overcome a trial after a prayer was offered up and answered, you grow in your faith. Walking by faith is contrary to walking by sight. When you walk by faith, you are completely trusting in the unseen, expecting God to deliver you or answer your prayer without having any sign of how it will happen. Experiencing the abundant blessings of God in ways that you could never imagine helps you to become a believer in the Almighty God. Women of faith all have similar characteristic traits. They are confident in the Lord, and they reminisce on what God has done for them in the past. When a new obstacle presents itself, instead of wallowing in doubt and despair, they begin to praise Him for what He has done in the past and gain reassurance that God is in control of the present. They begin to read the word of God and study experiences such as the story of the woman with the issue of blood where her faith and courage demonstrated complete trust in God, and it resulted in her cleanliness. Faith without works is dead. It is important to position yourself to receive the blessings of God despite what you are witnessing. There is nothing more powerful than a woman who resorts to prayer and at times even fast because she understands the power of having faith in a mighty God. In essence, faith is the key to answered prayers.

MY PRAYER CHALLENGE

Lord, help me to walk by faith and not by sight (2 Corinthians 5:7). Father, your word promises if I have faith the size of a mustard seed, I can move mountains. Father, please remove my fear and unbelief so that I can move mountains. Lord God, grant me the courage to trust you and be strong in the Lord. If I abide in Christ and I pray according to your will, I can ask anything in your name, and without a shadow of a doubt, it shall be mine! Lord, today, I pray for unshakeable faith, and I believe that faith is mine. Hallelujah!

ACTION PLAN:
WHAT IS YOUR NEXT STEP AS A WOMAN OF FAITH?

Lord, my desire is to_____

_____

_____

_____

_____

_____

_____

Lord, today, I make a commitment to _____

_____with the help of

the Holy Spirit.

Lord, to grow in my faith, I will_____

_____

_____

_____

_____

_____

_____

A WOMAN OF PRAYER

A nd all things, whatsoever ye shall ask in prayer, believing, ye shall receive (Matt 21:22, KJV).

The effectual fervent prayer of a righteous man availeth much (James 5:16, KJV).

Have you taken a moment to reflect on what prayer really is and why it is so powerful? "Prayer is a spiritual communion with God to earnestly petition, praise and offer thanks to God." Prayer brings us closer to God. When we earnestly petition God, amazing things happen; that's what makes prayer so powerful. Our Father says we have not because we ask not or we ask amiss (James 2:3). What does this mean? If we are truly walking by faith and we commune with our Father daily, we will know what to ask for, and He will give us the desires of our heart. It's not that the Lord doesn't already know our heart's desires or our needs. The truth is, He is our Creator, so He just wants us to draw close to Him so that we can trust in Him and lean not on our own understanding (Proverbs 4:5).

A BIBLICAL WOMAN OF PRAYER

Miraculous things happen when we pray. The story of Elkanah and Hannah in the Book of Samuel offers a good example of the power of prayer. Here, we find a married woman who was barren, unable to conceive a child. At the annual feast, she refused to eat but decided to pray to the Lord day and night so that He would bless her with a son. Hannah believed that God rewards those who diligently seek Him. She believed in the power of prayer. After many long nights and early mornings of weeping and prayer, she was blessed with a son. Not just any son, but because of her prayer, it was a son whose life was completely committed to the Lord. Samuel was a blessing to his mother, and he grew up to be a man of immeasurable faith who did astonishing things for the Lord. Hannah's prayer was answered. She believed, and she received.

Prayer is a powerful line of communication between our Heavenly Father above and us. It is so powerful that it changes things. It is the clear connection that gives us the opportunity to pour out our hearts without judgment and expect remarkable things from an awesome God.

We should always use this armor against the enemy to defeat discouragement or depression when facing trials and tribulations. Time and time again, I can testify to the power of answered prayer in my life and in the lives of others. People who are fortunate enough to experience the prayers of loved ones may even recover from illnesses faster than those who don't have any prayers in their lives. This is why the Bible exhorts us to pray one for another (James 5:16). There is real power in prayer.

A MODERN DAY WOMAN OF PRAYER

An example of prayer in action is a woman named Jennifer, whose son, Steven was in trouble with the law. Jennifer belonged to a prayer group that she regularly contacted for support when a crisis came up in her life or the lives of her loved ones. But this time, there wasn't even time to reach out to her group; her son informed her at the last minute that his court date had been moved up to the next day. Jennifer did not know what to do as the time approached. So, she stayed up most of the night praying, crying, and petitioning God for a favor for her son, claiming His promises through scriptures in hopes that the Lord would hear her prayers and answer as she asked. She believed that her Heavenly Father would soften the judge's heart and be merciful to her teenage son.

The next morning, Jennifer and Steven entered the courtroom and faced the judge, who appeared to have no mercy. Without his mercy, Steven was sure to go to prison or at least be sentenced to community service. Jennifer continued to have faith as she drew near to God, just as she had the night before in her prayers. Then suddenly, the judge's demeanor changed; he started talking with Steven like a son and giving him counsel on his actions and sharing future consequences that he would face if his behavior continued. Not long after, Steven's case was dismissed. Jennifer's prayers were answered. She could not help but rejoice in the courtroom after seeing what her prayers of faith had done for her son, Steven. Jennifer asked and believed that she would receive the blessings and favor of God, and her prayers were answered. She could now sing, "Victory is mine!" It was truly a day to remember.

HOW DO I BECOME A WOMAN OF PRAYER?

There are three simple things that you can do to become a woman of prayer. First, you must connect with God daily and pray without ceasing. I am not suggesting that you pray nonstop, but what I am suggesting is that every morning when you rise, throughout the day and before you lay your head to sleep, remember to pray. You do not need to be in a prostrate position or even on your knees to pray. For example, you could be leaving a department store when you unexpectedly stumble upon a final sale, and you pay way less than you expected in that moment. This would be a perfect moment to say, "Thank you for your favor, God!" Offering a short prayer of praise out loud or even in your head are opportunities to become a woman of prayer. Another simple prayer that you can recite in the Bible is the "Our Father Prayer" in Matthew 6:9-13. You can even rejoice by reciting the 23rd Psalms, an all-time favorite or a simple Psalm of praise such as Psalm 100 or Psalm 150.

Second, you need to change your perspective about God. You need to see God more as a friend that you have an intimate relationship with instead of some faraway being who is here to judge you and make your life difficult. When you think of one of your closest friends, you never feel like they are here to hurt you or make your life miserable, and you shouldn't view God in that manner either. God is here to help you to live life and live it more abundantly by providing you with His guidance and love.

Get a prayer partner or a prayer group. At times, life will knock you down, and you need a believer, someone with faith to intercede on your behalf or to pray with you to help you to get through these tough times. If you have a regular prayer partner or prayer group, you will not have to wait until you are in a critical situation to request prayer because you already have someone who is covering you in prayer and thinking of you. The Bible says where two or three are gathered; He is in their midst. Therefore, where there is much prayer, there is much power. You can never go wrong having others interceding on your behalf and praying with others for God to manifest Himself in your life.

Lastly, you need to read the word of God daily. Whether you want to read a chapter a day or study a specific book such as the Book of Ruth or Esther, you will become stronger in your walk with God as you read and study the word daily. You will begin to understand what God expects of you and who God really is. You can begin to pray the promises of God over your life with power. It is beneficial to invest in a study Bible so that you can have a detailed description of what your Bible is saying without getting stuck. I believe every woman should have a study bible. If your goal is to study and gain clarity of what God is teaching you, then you need a practical Bible to help you to reach your goal. Make God your friend and whisper to Him throughout the day what you are experiencing. Get into the habit of feeling comfortable with God and ask Him questions to guide your decision-making daily. Prayer is so powerful that even research studies have been able to demonstrate that people heal faster from illness when someone is praying for them. As you embark upon this journey, you will begin to believe more in the power of prayer. Whatever approach you decide, to become connected to the divine source, studying the Bible will help your prayer life in countless ways.

MY PRAYER CHALLENGE

Dear Lord, today, I pray that from this day onward, I will trust you in everything. I pray daily and believe the promises of the Lord, knowing that you will provide all of my needs and the needs of others. Lord, teach me how to cast my burdens at the altar and be confident that you will sustain me in every possible way. Father, I know that you love me more than anything and your desire is that I draw close to you. Father, help me to remember that my problems are never too big for you to bear if I trust you with all of my heart, mind, and soul. Father, today, I pray that I am able to let go, and let God in Jesus' Name. Amen.

ACTION PLAN:
WHAT IS YOUR NEXT STEP AS A WOMAN OF PRAYER?

Lord, my desire is to_____

_____

_____

_____

_____

_____

_____

Lord, today, I make a commitment to _____

_____with the help of

the Holy Spirit.

Lord to grow in my prayer life, I will_____

_____

_____

_____

_____

_____

_____

QUALITY #3
A WOMAN OF PRAISE

I n everything give thanks: for this is the will of God in Christ Jesus concerning you (1 Thessalonians 5:18, KJV).

Have you noticed how easy it is to find fault or complain about everything? Think about it: someone could be sharply dressed from head to toe, and your eyes will focus on the small smudge on his or her shirt. Our eyes are trained to immediately zero in on faults; we have a propensity to focus on what's wrong. It doesn't matter how many goals we have achieved; we focus on that one unachievable goal or failure. Why is that? We need to learn to live with an attitude of gratitude. Instead of emphasizing on the negative, we need to retrain our minds to give thanks for how God has blessed us with so many good things. Many of us have all of our senses, good health, jobs to go to, homes to shelter us, family, friends, and so much more. Yet, the most important things seem so small, and the least important things appear so significant. Where does it end?

To learn how to give thanks in everything, we need to start by thanking God even when we don't have much. Because if we can't learn to be faithful with few things, how can our Father bless us with many things? If it is according to His will, you will have it in His time. Thank Him for patience even when you are having a difficult time waiting on the Lord. Thank Him for being a rewarder of those who diligently seek Him. Thank Him for working all things together for good in your life. We must learn to claim His promises and keep them close to our hearts. Are you starting to get the flow of this? You can turn any bad situation into a good one, and any bad day into a good one if you learn to consistently focus on the positive instead of the negative. This may not be easy to do at first, but with practice, it will become a normal routine, just like anything else in your life. I love the simple analogy of the glass of water that can be perceived as half empty or half full. Some may even see beyond the glass and envision that it is overflowing. Your perception of the glass is a reflection of how you think in your everyday life. We should learn to see our lives overflowing with blessings and know that God will move mountains just for us. He is an awesome God! We must change our thinking and start having an attitude of gratitude.

A BIBLICAL WOMAN OF PRAISE

We all go through struggles and at times, we may feel that there is no reason to give praise and thanks. The biblical story of Anna, the prophetess, touches my heart. The second chapter of Luke captures Anna's life in three compelling verses. Anna was blessed with a husband for seven years. She then became a widow for 84 years. The Bible does not give details on how her husband died, but it does place great emphasis on Anna's attitude after the loss of her husband. She was never described as a bitter woman who cursed God. She was a woman who chose to praise God in all her years of widowhood. She departed not from the temple but served God with fasting and prayer day and night. This woman still found a reason to praise God and give Him thanks. In Anna's life, we celebrate a woman of great faith, service, prayer, and obedience; a woman who understood how to give praise and thanks in everything. What an awesome story of a woman seeking after God's own heart!

A MODERN DAY WOMAN OF PRAISE

I realized just how much I take for granted when our Women's Ministries Group in the local area sponsored some orphaned children in Tanzania, Africa. Through this ministry, we had the opportunity to help children who couldn't help themselves. Many of these children have absolutely no living relatives. Their relatives died from war, AIDS, or some form of illness or disease due to malnutrition. They did not have the resources to seek the medical attention they needed. Can you imagine waking up to the reality that all of your family members are gone? Not just your mother and father but your siblings, your aunts, your uncles, your cousins —everyone. There are children facing that dilemma every day. Do you see why you have a lot to be thankful for? Working with these children convicted me not to focus on what I *don't* have but to focus on the many blessings that I *do* have. You may not have the best family, but at least, you have a family. There are many people who would love to trade places with you. Your parents may not be perfect and may not have done the best job raising you, but praise God; you didn't have to raise yourself. The Lord is looking for us to give thanks in whatever state we are in, whether we have one million dollars or one dollar; whether we have a lot or a little, He wants us to be content (Philippians 4:11).

It is virtually impossible to be positive and negative at the same time; one thought will dominate the other. Let's try to give thanks unto the Lord and sing praises unto His name (Psalms 92:1) in the big and small blessings of life and remember that we are blessed and highly favored!

HOW DO I BECOME A WOMAN OF PRAISE?

Ladies, the good news is, becoming a woman of praise does not require any special formula; you just have to get into the habit of praising. When you wake up in the morning, praise God for waking up! When you get to work, praise God for having a job! When you eat breakfast, lunch or dinner, praise God for having a meal! When you make it home from work, praise God for His traveling mercies! When you have a trial that you are facing, praise God through the trial! The word of God tells us in I Thessalonians 5:18 that, in everything, give thanks because this is the will of God. When you praise God, the enemy flees because he is not able to handle you singing praises to our Lord and Savior. Embracing an attitude of gratitude is a key element to chase away negative emotions. You can share a personal, heartfelt prayer of gratitude where you can be more specific and find at least five things to thank or praise God for daily. It can be as simple as waking you up each morning in good health, shelter, family, friends, a job, and helping you to make it through another day.

Another approach is to get sticky notes and write on your mirror in various places throughout your home, office or even in your car to remind you to sing praises to the Most High. When you start praising God in the simple things, it will become so natural to praise Him in everything. Praise is what we must do to keep depression, doubt, negativity, fear, and anxiety away. You can be assured that no matter what condition you were in before you began praising God, you will feel much better afterward. There are certain books of the Bible, with the Psalm of David being one of them, that can assist you in praising God. There is something profound about singing praises to the Most High God. If you don't believe me, try it for yourself. You will definitely feel the power of praise and will soon realize what you have been missing out on all of these years!

MY PRAYER CHALLENGE

Lord, I pray that I am a woman of praise and worship. I want to praise you throughout the storms of life and share my testimony with others. God, give me a heart of contentment and teach me how to give thanks in everything. I bless the Lord at all times; your praise is continually in my mouth (Psalms 34:1). Lord, I praise you morning, noon and night. Lord, I honor you and uplift your name. Father God, help me to edify other women, men, children, and families and no longer be double-minded in any of my ways. Help me to remember that the Lord loves me and "every good gift and every perfect gift is from above" (James 1:17). Lord, help me to be a true worshiper. Father God, today I celebrate you, I adore you, I worship you, and I praise you. In Jesus' Name, Amen.

ACTION PLAN:
WHAT IS YOUR NEXT STEP AS A WOMAN OF PRAISE?

Lord, my desire is to_____

_____

_____

_____

_____

_____

_____

Lord, today, I make a commitment to _____

_____with the help of

the Holy Spirit.

Lord to grow in praise, I will_____

_____

_____

_____

_____

_____

_____

QUALITY #4
A WOMAN OF LOVE

Love... always protects, always trusts, always hopes, and always perseveres. Love never fails (1 Corinthians 13:7, 8; NIV).

Love is the ultimate gift that we can freely express and give. We have seen the ultimate sacrifice of love through our Father sending His only begotten Son to die for our sins.

THE GREATEST LOVE OF ALL

Did you know that the most important attribute anyone can have is love?

(You can prophesy in my name...but without love you have nothing...(1 Corinthians 13:2). This means you can have everything tangible in this world and yet have nothing. Many people use this expressive word, *love*, very loosely, without recognizing how deep it is. So, what is love? Good question; I'm glad you asked. "God is love, love suffereth long, love is kind, love envieth not, and love is not puffed up" (1Corinthians 13:4). What better demonstration of love than what our Heavenly Father poured out on us, in sending His only begotten Son into the world to die a grueling death on the cross, not to condemn the world but so that the world can be saved (John 3:17). Once you understand that God's love is everything you need, you have begun living life to the fullest. God wants us to love one another as Christ loves us. He never said that our brethren would not make us angry. What He did say was, be ye angry and sin not (Ephesians 4:26). He knows that being around people all the time can bring out the worst in them and even in you. Our ability or inability to love has a direct correlation to how we were raised and what we were taught. It also reflects the relationship we have with Christ.

Our Heavenly Father could not have offered us a better illustration of earthly love between man and woman than the union of marriage. The relationship between husband and wife is one of the best relationships a man and woman could ever have to build character, strength, and patience. Marriage is a lifelong commitment. You should never allow your eagerness to leave your parents' home, the need for stability or the ambiance of the wedding day to overshadow the qualities that are absent from your significant other. Make this choice carefully and seek many counselors of great wisdom and experience. Start praying like you have never done before. Before you say, "I do," remember your wedding vows are not just a commitment to your spouse, they are also to the Lord.

A MODERN DAY WOMAN OF LOVE

There is no selfishness in love. One of the greatest human examples of love that I have witnessed is my mother's love for my father. My mother was in her late 20s when she married my father, who was 11 years older than she was. She was running away from a verbally abusive father who was not the kindest man to his wife (my grandmother). She ran into the arms of a man who in many ways displayed the same behaviors that her dad did. My dad came from a family that was well-off, while my mom came from a deprived family. My dad never had a role model in his father to recognize that a father is more than just a man who takes good care of his children, but he should also be a good husband who takes good care of his wife.

My mother was excited to marry my dad, whose family's wealth seemed to hold the promise of a better future. But it came at a great price. My dad never followed his family tradition of completing dental school because he already had the trade from his earlier years of life. My dad never ended up wealthy as his father and siblings were. My mom spent many sleepless nights striving to better herself by going back to school, working full time, and raising six children. She also raised my dad's children from a previous marriage and tolerated his extramarital affairs. My mom prayed daily and hoped that one day, things would be different. She suffered mistreatment for many years, but she endured this pain with meekness. She never complained. Only after my siblings and I were grown did she open up and share with us about our father's infidelity and the emotional distress she suffered at his hand.

As the years went by, my dad became ill and could no longer take care of himself. The same wife whom he mistreated was the one who now took care of him. My mom could have used this as an opportunity to retaliate and seek revenge, but even with all the pain and hurt that she had endured over the years, she still took good care of my father.

Three years before my dad passed away, he committed his life to Christ and got baptized. Without my mom's selflessness and commitment to her marriage, it's doubtful that he would have ever experienced a love that would spark his desire to give his life to Christ. And yet, my mom still struggled with her silent pain. She harbored a spirit of unforgiveness toward my dad for years, not knowing if she could ever let it go.

During the last months of my father's life, my mom finally let go and let God. She went to the hospital day and night to be by my father's side. She read the Bible to him, and they prayed and talked with each other. It was as if they had rekindled an old flame and nothing but the time that remained mattered. Now, years after his death, mom still feels the sting of the hurtful past and healing is a daily struggle, but despite her pain, we strongly believe her testimony of love won my father's soul to the kingdom. Through her love, loyalty and commitment to the Lord and her wedding vows, she fulfilled her marital and Christian duties, which were binding until death, whether in sickness or in health.

Since every situation differs due to various circumstances, this path may not be the path for every woman to take without seeking a multitude of counselors—first beginning with our Heavenly Father. However, it was the path that my mom took, and I celebrate her today for being an honorable woman who kept her marriage vows in the best times and in the worst times.

Many of us fail to realize that sickness is not just physical. Countless homes are broken, and children are growing up with an emotional pain that is much deeper than physical pain. My mom and dad were married for 44 years. It was a difficult, painful marriage for my mom, but with the fruits of the spirit—love, joy, peace, longsuffering, gentleness, goodness, faith, meekness and temperance the Lord's will was done.

DO I BECOME A WOMAN OF LOVE?

First and foremost, we must know what love is. The Bible tells us in I John 4:8 ...God is love. When God is not the divine source in your life, then you are most likely walking in lust, not love. Love is kind, selfless, not boastful, and respectful; love listens to the needs and wants of others and is accommodating; love is healthy and brings out the best in each person even though you may still experience growing pains. Love is consistent, committed, caring, truthful, safe and giving. Love is persevering, and love never fails. Quite often, we misinterpret love, so it is hard to become a woman of love. It is important to understand what love is and what love is not. Society often confuses love and lust. Lust is controlling, unkind, selfish, manipulative, inconsistent, possessive, unfaithful, intentionally hurtful, untruthful, unsafe, and uncommitted. It brings out the worst in people.

Gaining the right perspective of love is the first step to becoming a woman of love. The second step is operationalizing love. When you look at Jesus' ministry on Earth, He met the needs of people, and He was authentic. Remember, love is a verb. It is action-oriented. Love is not just a word that you say; it is a behavior that you demonstrate to help others feel loved in your presence. One chapter you should read daily is 1st Corinthians 13—the love chapter. This chapter will be a daily reminder of what love is. You can also do small selfless acts every chance you get where there is no reward in it for you. Demonstrate love in your actions by helping others at times in a sacrificial way. Love is not always easy, and at times, we may even feel that some people are unlovable, and not worthy of our service, but we need to remember to put ourselves in the same category. As sinners, we were not worth saving either, but yet, Jesus loved us so

36

much that He stood in the gap as our substitute and died to save us so that we could have life and have it more abundantly. This is truly a love story and the reason everyone deserves to experience love, starting with you!

MY PRAYER CHALLENGE

Lord, teach me how to be selfless, and love unconditionally. Holy Spirit, I give you permission to intercede on my behalf, to help me endure injury with patience, and without resentment. Give me a spirit of gentleness and humility. Father, I pray for understanding. I realize that You will never give me more than I can bear, nor will you ever take me to anything that You do not already have a plan to bring me through (I Cor. 10:13). Father, today, I declare that I am a woman of love and I give you all the honor, glory and the praise for changing my heart. In Jesus' Name, Amen.

ACTION PLAN:
WHAT IS YOUR NEXT STEP AS A WOMAN OF LOVE?

Lord, my desire is to_____

_____

_____

_____

_____

_____

_____

Lord, today, I make a commitment to _____

_____with the help of

the Holy Spirit.

Lord to grow in love, I will_____

_____

_____

_____

_____

_____

_____

QUALITY #5
A WOMAN OF FORGIVENESS

And forgive us our debts, as we forgive our debtors (Matthew 6:12, KJV).

Every day, we choose whether or not we want to be happy or sad, mad or glad. We decide what our day will be like, how much time we want to invest in our relationships, and what goals we want to accomplish. Yet, we have no control over bad things happening to good people. All too often, we hear about the faithful wife who is everything a man could ask for, and is still abandoned by her husband for another woman; or the innocent child who is physically or emotionally abused by his parents or relatives; or the young lady jogging in the park who is assaulted and raped. We will always wrestle with unanswered questions until we get to heaven and have the privilege of asking God Himself, but while we are here, we need to make the best of it.

Let's take a moment to reflect on how we forgive others since it is correlated to how the Lord forgives us. Remember, Jesus made a commitment to us in the Lord's Prayer: "forgive your brethren of their trespasses as our heavenly Father will forgive us of our trespasses" (Matthew 6:14). This is a conditional promise. How can we expect God to forgive us when we are not forgiving? He has provided us many counsels on forgiveness because He understands our nature. The human side of us always wants to retaliate, hold a grudge, and recall the offense by saying, "I will forgive, but I can't forget." God says when He forgives us, He casts our sins into the bottom of the sea; He brings them back no more. Our Father does not want you to take matters into your own hands. This is why Jesus said when He was suffering on the

41

cross; Father forgive them; for they know not what they are doing (Luke 23:34). Do you really think that a person could see the pain that he or she is inflicting on family members and loved ones and still consciously choose eternal death over eternal life? We are often so busy being the victim that we don't think about the fact that the perpetrator needs a saving relationship with Jesus Christ in his or her life, just as we do.

Sometimes, a fellow Christian is the one who does the most hurtful things to you and your first thought may be: "and she calls herself a Christian." Remember, we "have all sinned and fallen short of the glory of God" (Romans 3:23).

Forgiveness is one of the most difficult processes to master. Just when you think you have finally overcome in one situation, another one presents itself to remind you that there is still much you can learn.

A BIBLICAL STORY OF FORGIVENESS

The story of Hosea and Gomer is one of the greatest biblical examples of forgiveness in the Bible. Hosea, a faithful man of God, was instructed by the Lord to marry a prostitute, who was chronically unfaithful. She didn't spare him any shame. She cheated on him, bore children out of wedlock, and prostituted herself for riches. She inflicted this shame on her husband and the family name without any signs of remorse. Hosea could have left her on countless occasions, but he endured through the pain and agony of his wife's unfaithfulness, and he loved her unconditionally. The story ends with Gomer finally returning to her husband as he patiently waited for her return and had unwavering faith that she would eventually turn back to God. This was an act of faithfulness to their marriage vows and God. Love is kind and forgiving. Love is not based on the other person's actions towards us; it is a symbol of our love for Christ. When we forgive those who hurt us, we are telling God that we love Him so much that we are not willing to let anything or anyone get in the way of our relationship with Him. Ladies, if the story was reversed and Gomer was the one who had experienced infidelity at the hands of Hosea, would you be able to forgive your husband the way that Hosea forgave his wife?

If you are still struggling to understand why forgiveness is so important, try looking at it from Christ's perspective. Can you imagine what Christ went through for us on earth? He was rejected by the very people He came to save; denied by His own disciple; laughed at; spat upon; and finally, crucified in cold blood. Can you imagine going through something this severe with a spirit of forgiveness toward the perpetrators, even *while* it was happening? This is the ultimate sacrifice that was made for you and me, and yet we walk around as though other people do not deserve forgiveness. If we are honest with ourselves, we would be able to realize that we are the ones that do not deserve forgiveness but it was granted to us anyway. Let's keep petitioning the Lord in prayer with the help and guidance of the Holy Spirit to soften our hearts so that we can forgive others as we have been forgiven.

A MODERN DAY WOMAN OF FORGIVENESS

A woman that I greatly admire is an inspiring author. This woman of forgiveness has blessed my life over the years with her powerful ministry of writing prayer books. She is a great example of forgiveness and the power that is within us when we let go and allow God. This woman did not have an easy childhood. Actually, she grew up with a mentally ill mother who was abusive in many ways. She suffered isolation and was locked in a closet quite often in her childhood by her mom with no help or protection from her father who worked long hours. Due to her traumatic childhood for many years, she suffered from depression, fear, anxiety, anger, feelings of hopelessness and helplessness. She began drinking heavily and used drugs while engaged in many other self-destructive behaviors. At one point, she felt like death was the only way out. In the midst of one of the worst times of her life, the Lord sent a friend to visit her. She then met a Pastor who introduced her to Jesus in a way that she had never experienced before. As she read religious books including the Gospel of John referred by the Pastor, she began finding a new life in Christ Jesus. Her hope was no longer in a life of despair but in a God who had great plans for her life and future. This was when she learned about the power of prayer and the amazing things that happen when we pray. Her new revelation transformed her life and the lives of countless others through her profound books on prayer. Throughout this transformation, this woman of forgiveness realized she could not harbor unforgiveness towards her mother. While it was a process that took time, she was able to forgive her mother, her father and forgive herself for any self-destruction and bless the lives of millions of women including me.

Ladies, we cannot afford to hold onto unforgiveness and miss out on the blessings that God has in store for our lives. When we walk in a spirit of unforgiveness, it is no different than locking ourselves in a prison and waiting for someone else to let us out when we are the only person with the key to free ourselves. Unforgiveness is not easy by any means, this is why Jesus advised Peter to forgive seventy times seven to make a point that it is a process that takes time. Whether you are struggling to forgive your parents, yourself, people in a past relationship, a family member, a boss, co-worker, ex-friend or enemy, remember you hold the key to forgiveness.

Love is a sacrifice. If we say we love Christ, we have to learn to forgive our brethren no matter what. Forgiveness is a healing process. God knows that at times, we will get angry and be hurt, but He says, "Commit your way to the Lord; trust also in him; and he shall bring it to pass" (Psalms 37:5, AKJV).

HOW DO I BECOME A WOMAN OF FORGIVENESS?

Ladies, I just want to be transparent with you, becoming a woman of forgiveness is one of the hardest things to do outside of having a heart of love for everyone. I believe the two are closely related. To love someone unconditionally, you need to constantly forgive them for what they have done or may continually do. I think quite often; we have the wrong impression of forgiveness. We often feel like if we forgive someone, that we are excusing their unacceptable behavior and giving them a pass. However, forgiveness has nothing to do with the other person, but it has everything to do with you. It's like being imprisoned, and you have the key to open the prison gate, but you are waiting for someone else to unlock the prison door on the outside. Once you realize that forgiveness is a decision that you make to let go and let God soften your heart towards the other person, you have begun the process of forgiveness. Even when you tell yourself you forgive the person or even forgive yourself, there may be times that the incident replays itself in your mind and you may find yourself getting angry all over again. At this point, what you need to do is stop and pray and ask God to remove the feelings you are harboring for the other person or the guilt and shame you are feeling about yourself.

Forgiveness is a process that occurs over time, and you will go through several emotions, and you may experience this for some time when you see the person or have a reminder of the incident. Forgiveness does not mean that you place yourself in the same vulnerable situation again to experience similar pain, but it means that you are wiping the slate clean and allowing a new beginning to occur. I must admit that I am speaking to myself today as I have struggled with unforgiveness in the past as well. Remember the power of prayer and laying your burdens at the altar and leaving them there. Also, remember that whatever wrong we have experienced, Jesus paid it all. Jesus died a brutal death on the cross and endured pain and suffering to save us all even though we were undeserving. We should remind ourselves of this priceless act when we feel someone does not deserve forgiveness. While it may not be easy to forgive, a courageous approach that may be helpful would be to speak with the person who wronged you face to face to reconcile, but unfortunately, this is not always possible depending on the situation especially if the person is deceased or unwilling. If it is possible and you are up for it, I encourage you to speak with them and let them know how violated you feel and how hurt you are. Be specific without attacking the other person. You are merely sharing the truth from your perspective about what happened and sharing a heartfelt testimony of how you feel about what happened. You can express yourself by saying I feel sad, angry, disrespected, etc.)

Another approach is to write a letter to finally release the things that you want to get off your chest about the person and the situation, and either mail it to yourself, tear it up or burn it. Just releasing everything that you ever wanted to say to the person is therapeutic even if the other person never reads it. Lastly, you can give yourself a time window of 3 hours, one day, two days, or even a week, and vent about it as much as possible and once that time window that you designated ends, make a promise to yourself that you will not bring it up again. You may have another approach that works for you, if it is working, use it. There is no one size fits all approach to forgiveness. You may find yourself using several approaches to get through this. There are extenuating circumstances when the situation may be ongoing, and you may have to endure long-suffering for quite some time and the Bible helps to give us counsel on this. If it is too much to bear you may have to resort to prayer and fasting or even seek professional counseling/therapy to gain the strength needed to move forward. On the cross, Jesus said, forgive them Father, for they know not what they do. You may be saying to yourself they know exactly what they are doing. Some of these situations that I am referencing may be some form of abuse, molestation or mistreatment in a relationship. While you may feel that on the surface the person knows what they are doing, I really want to believe if people truly knew Jesus and if they knew how much pain they are causing the other person, they would not continue these heinous acts. Remember, what does not destroy you will make you stronger. This is now a part of your life testimony and story, and it can empower you as well as others when you share it.

MY PRAYER CHALLENGE

Dear God, help me to die to self daily. Teach me O Lord how to walk in a spirit of forgiveness and forgive my debtors as you forgave me. Lord, my desire is to be a living testimony for you. Help me to forgive others and forgive myself for the sins that easily beset me. Father God, since your Son Jesus died to save me from my sins and gave me the free gift of salvation when I was undeserving, help me to freely forgive my brethren." Father, today, I declare that I am a woman of forgiveness in Jesus' Name, Amen.

ACTION PLAN:
WHAT IS YOUR NEXT STEP AS A WOMAN OF FORGIVENESS?

Lord, my desire is to_____

_____

_____

_____

_____

_____

Lord, today, I make a commitment to _____

_____with the help of

the Holy Spirit.

Lord to grow in forgiveness, I will _____

_____

_____

_____

_____

_____

_____

QUALITY #6
A WOMAN OF PATIENCE

Knowing this, that the trying of your faith worketh patience (James 1:3, KJV).

According to the American Institute of Stress, over 60% of chronic illnesses are stress related, not to mention that stress increases your chance of getting heart disease, heart attacks, and strokes. When we maintain high levels of stress, it disturbs our inner and outer peace, interferes with our mental health and causes us to no longer trust in what God can do in our lives. Often times, we want answers and refuse to patiently wait on the Lord to allow the situation to come to pass.

I am sure we can all testify to the level of frustration that we feel at times when we are waiting for God's answer to a specific situation. You see, no signs of what you have been fervently praying about. You have petitioned God, cried out; you even had prayer warriors pray for you over this matter time and time again but NO signs. To top it all, at a time like this, the Lord may decide to be silent. You can no longer hear Him speak to you. This is a true test of your faith. He wants to see if you will doubt Him, if you will interfere with His master plan, if you will turn your back on Him and try to do His job. God promised that He will not withhold any good gifts from His children; and if we truly believe the promises of God, why do we walk around hopelessly, fearfully, or doubtfully? Our Father is a God of hope, faith, and belief, so anything contrary to this is not of God. God's word never returns void (Isaiah 55:11).

On our journey through life, we will go through valleys of darkness before we get to the mountaintop. God is teaching us how to be patient and find peace in spite of the size of the storm, failures, disappointments or unexplainable circumstances. Throughout this process, our faith will be tried, but by waiting patiently on the Lord, we will be refined, and our faith will be strengthened.

A BIBLICAL WOMAN OF PATIENCE

There is a parable about a nameless widow in Luke 18:1-8. What makes this woman worth mentioning is that she was determined. She did not just sit around waiting for something to happen, she was proactive. She is a great example and teacher of patience and perseverance in prayer. While her name was never mentioned, there are several things that we know about this woman. We are aware that she had experienced an injustice by the hands of an unjust judge and she did not just sit around and watch this happen. While the parable never mentioned what the injustice was, we know that the unnamed widow had to deal with a judge who did not fear God neither did he regard man. There could be countless reasons that this woman experienced an injustice by a secular judge, but one thing is for sure, she wore this judge out. She kept troubling him and coming into his courtroom despite whatever harsh consequences she could face for harassment. The judge finally said, while I do not fear God nor regard man, give this woman justice because she keeps coming before me and she is wearing me out. This woman patiently waited on the Lord to answer her prayer despite all of the odds against her. God showed up and showed out!

A woman connected to the Divine Source realizes that in challenging times, she has to trust God and her relationship with the Lord grows deeper because it is only by His grace that her strength is renewed daily. Nonetheless, even great women of God waver in their faith when they have to patiently wait on the Lord. At times, you may think about taking matters into your own hands, but unfortunately, you may experience the negative consequence of impatience due to the lack of trust in the Lord. This comes to light when we acknowledge that with man, it is impossible, but with God, all things are possible (Matt 19:26). What an awesome God we serve!

A MODERN DAY WOMAN OF PATIENCE

So many of us single ladies experience a lack of patience when it comes to waiting on our husband, the King that God is preparing for us. It is the enemy's plan that you become anxious so that you can walk outside of God's plan for your life and end up with the wrong mate. His goal is to destroy the ministry that you are supposed to have in your marriage that God has been preparing you for your whole life.

One young lady I know was dating a guy she thought she would marry. She just knew he was the one. He was a professed Christian and active in ministry—a leader in his church. He knew the Word backward and forward, but his life testimony did not align with who he claimed to be. In the end, all she was left with was a broken heart and a relationship that led to a dead end. She finally realized this relationship was in the flesh, not in the spirit and there was no truth in it. They were not compatible after all. This wasn't what the Lord had in store for her. She was misled by her heart's desire to be married. Today, she always testifies of how "God is so good!" She had to learn to let go and let God. This was definitely a process that did not occur overnight. Currently, she is married with children, and she has realized that waiting patiently on the Lord was the best way. We also must allow the Lord to lead us to the relationship that would be a marriage of ministry. Let's allow the Lord to become the center of our lives, and there is no doubt in my mind that in God's timing, wedding bells will be ringing! This will be a day to rejoice!

Ladies, we must be careful of being too anxious to be married. Our Father says be anxious for nothing. This only allows the devil room to lead attractively packaged counterfeits into our lives. If you resist the devil, he will flee from you, but if you place any gods before God in your life, even the desire to be married can become an obsession in your life, granting the enemy power to deceive you. When you let go and let God, following His lead, you can't go wrong.

Despite how you may feel now, it is much better to be happily single than unhappily married. So, take your time. You only live once, and you may live to be married for more years than you are single. Hence, enjoy your single years, which are a gift from the Lord and prepare for the blessing of marriage. Allow God to lead the right person into your life, but first, you must trust Him in this area and every other area of your life.

HOW DO I BECOME A WOMAN OF PATIENCE?

Becoming a woman of patience is a prayerful process. Honestly, I am still a work in progress in this area of my life just as many of you are. When you feel like you have mastered patience in one area, the Lord will quickly reveal other areas to demonstrate that there is still some growing to do. As you develop your prayer life and increase your faith, patience develops simultaneously. When God delays His answers to our prayers, it is often for our own good. Nonetheless, the unknown has never been easy for many of us to handle. There are several methods that you can implement to help with becoming a woman of patience.

The Bible is a comforting source to read to help you to learn how to wait patiently on the Lord. Reading many of the biblical stories and quoting God's promises are great ways to gain reassurance. Recognizing what God has done for His children in the past and what He can do for you in the present is extremely uplifting. Another approach is to record your testimonies in a journal. Writing down what God has brought you through can be exactly what you need in your weakest moments to increase your faith and patience as you keep moving forward. Trusting the Lord's timing is important. Lastly, surrounding yourself with other God-fearing people who are willing to share their testimonies to help you to gain a boost to persevere to the end. At times, when we just pause for a moment, take three deep breaths and remember what God has done for us in the past can help to subside any worry, fear or impatience and redirect us to think about how we felt after God proved us wrong and we learned that we didn't have anything to worry about after all.

MY PRAYER CHALLENGE

Lord, help me to acquire the patience that I need to surrender my life to you and submit to your timing. Father, give me the patience to wait on your answers and rest assured that at the appointed time, the answers will come. Lord, help me to believe wholeheartedly that if I delight myself in you, you will give me the desires of my heart (Psalm 37:4). Today, I declare that I am a woman of patience in Jesus' Name, Amen.

ACTION PLAN:
WHAT IS YOUR NEXT STEP AS
PATIENCE?

Lord, my desire is to_____

_____

_____

_____

_____

_____

_____

Lord, today, I make a commitment to _____
_____with the help of
the Holy Spirit.

Lord to grow in my patience, I will_____

_____

_____

_____

_____

_____

_____

QUALITY #7
A WOMAN OF WISDOM

Forsake her not, and she shall preserve thee: love her, and she shall keep thee. Wisdom is the principal thing; therefore get wisdom: and with all thy getting get understanding (Proverbs 3:6-7, KJV)

The Book of Proverbs is one of the most recognized books of the Bible. There are so many lessons to learn and apply to our own lives. How often do we neglect the counsel that Solomon has shared with us from his own life experience? When we begin to recognize that it is much better to gain wisdom than silver or gold, we have just begun walking in the fear of the Lord. Heavenly wisdom far supersedes any earthly knowledge or wisdom that we could acquire. When we walk in the fear of the Lord, we are seeking heavenly wisdom, which is a priceless treasure. It doesn't matter how many degrees you obtain in this life, how brilliant you are, or how eloquent you may speak, what really matters is that you are walking in the fear of the Lord (Proverbs 9:10).

A BIBLICAL WOMAN OF WISDOM

One such woman was Abigail. We find her story in 1 Samuel 25. She was the wife of a rich man named Nabal. Her character illustrates womanhood after the order of Christ. Abigail was a woman of beautiful countenance and great wisdom. Her husband was just the opposite. His name meant folly was with him and he was known to be churlish and evil. Nabal's only thoughts were of satisfying his own appetite. He had no gratitude toward God—he sought only to glorify himself.

David had helped Nabal's herdsmen when they were in need, so when David's men needed food as they passed through Nabal's territory; he expected the favor to be returned. David sent 10 of his men to greet Nabal in peace and kindly ask him for food. Nabal refused because of his evil heart, and David grew angry. He was prepared to lead his men to take Nabal's life and destroy his household. When Abigail heard what Nabal had done, she took responsibility for his thoughtless actions. She gathered 200 loaves, 200 cakes of figs, 100 clusters of raisins, two bottles of wine, five sheep, and five measures of parched corn and laid them on donkeys. Her servants went before her, and she met David and his men on a covert hill. There she fell at David's feet, condemning Nabal's brutality and foolishness.

Despite the abuse Abigail would have to come home and face, she would not consider anything less than complete obedience to God. Under tremendous pressure, she remained a saint. She remained faithful to her marriage vows but continued to walk in the fear of the Lord. Ten days after her return, the Lord smote Nabal, and he died. Abigail's obedience prevented David and his men from committing murder, and the revenge was the Lord's. Abigail's faithfulness was rewarded, and David soon took her as his wife. Abigail was indeed a woman who walked in the fear of the Lord and a woman to be praised!

A MODERN DAY WOMAN OF WISDOM

Many of you have heard of the well-known Civil Rights leader, Dr. Martin Luther King jr. who fought for equal rights for African-Americans through non-violence practices. I would like to suggest that behind every wise man, there is a wise woman. That woman was Coretta Scott King. As an author, singer, activist, civil rights leader and the wife of Dr. Martin Luther King jr., Coretta played a prominent role in the Civil Rights Movement in the 1960s. After the death of her husband in 1968, she continued to fight for equal rights for African-Americans and became a part of the Women's Movement. She also founded the King Center and sought to make his birthday a national holiday. Coretta continued to fight for equal rights until her death in January 2006. She was inducted into the Alabama Women's Hall of Fame and has been called the "First Lady of the Civil Rights Movement." This wise Christian woman did not allow her husband's tragic death to create fear or anxiety in her because her faith and confidence was in the Lord. When we seek counsel and understanding from the Lord and remember that "the wisdom that is from above is first pure, then peaceable, gentle and easy to be entreated, full of mercy, fruits, without partiality and without hypocrisy. And the fruit of righteousness is sown in peace of them that make peace (James 3:17,18)." Coretta has demonstrated the wisdom of the Lord through her patience, love, perseverance, humility, and the life-changing impact that she has made on the society. This couple's ministry will forever be remembered for changing the world in love. When you are called by God to do a great work, your wisdom comes from the Lord. I am thankful that there are still people around that are willing to sacrifice their lives for the freedom of others and I look forward to thanking this lovely couple when we get to the kingdom for their fearless life-changing ministry.

Ladies, at times, life may appear perplexing. We may believe that we are on the right path; we may seek earthly knowledge only to realize that it is contrary to the word of God. We must continually pray for a spirit of discernment and ask God to give us wisdom in all things. Therefore, we need the word of God engraved in our hearts. We must recognize that we may be successful for a time, but if we turn away from God's counsel, we too will fall.

HOW DO I BECOME A WOMAN OF WISDOM?

Becoming a woman of wisdom is understanding the importance of hearing the voice of the Lord and being obedient to His voice. James 1:5 says, "If any of you lack wisdom, let him ask of God that giveth to all men freely." It is important to be clear that we can always seek God's counsel and study the word of God to gain understanding. The Bible speaks about wisdom often and emphasizes how important it is to have it so we should take it very seriously. Be careful who you seek counsel from because you can seek wisdom from different people in different areas of your life, but you need to hear God's voice clearly to know who to go to for what areas. It is important to not just read God's word but study it to gain clarity so that you can make wise decisions. Pray fervently to make sure that the counsel you are receiving is indeed from the Lord. Happy is the man that finds wisdom and gets understanding (Proverbs 3:13). If you feel uneasy about your decision and you don't feel like it is in line with the word of God, this may be a time to be still and wait to receive confirmation from the Lord. Quite often, we end up with regret because we make quick irrational decisions. Lastly, never trust your feelings alone because your feelings are unstable. Seek Godly counsel, and be not wise in thine own eyes; fear the Lord, and depart from evil (Proverbs 3:7).

MY PRAYER CHALLENGE

Father, teach me how to trust in the Lord with all of my heart and lean not on my own understanding. Teach me to acknowledge you in all my ways and allow you to direct my path (Proverbs 3:5-6). Help me to believe that you always know best, even when I can't see it. You are the Alpha and the Omega, the beginning and the end, the first and the last (Revelation 22:13). You are Omnipotent. Today, I declare that I am a woman of wisdom. Thank you, Father, for hearing and answering my prayer in Jesus' Name, Amen.

ACTION PLAN:
WHAT IS YOUR NEXT STEP AS A WOI
WISDOM?

Lord, my desire is to_____

_____

_____

_____

_____

_____

_____

Lord, today, I make a commitment to _____

_____with the help of

the Holy Spirit.

Lord to grow in my wisdom, I will_____

_____

_____

_____

_____

_____

_____

QUALITY #8
A WOMAN OF OBEDIENCE

Every good gift and every perfect gift is from above, and cometh down from the Father of lights, with whom is no variableness, neither shadow of turning (James 1:17, KJV).

If you fully obey the LORD your God and carefully follow all his commands I give you today, the LORD your God will set you high above all the nations on earth (Deuteronomy 28:1, NLT).

Throughout God's word, there are conditional and unconditional promises made to God's children. The unconditional promises are promises that God follows through on just because He loves us and there is no particular requirement on our behalf, but then there are conditional promises that indicate if we obey God in a specific way, God will bless us in a specific way. Today, we want to focus on a woman of obedience. Being a woman of obedience does not come naturally to us because we are self-serving creatures. We want to serve the flesh and please self first. However, when we walk in the flesh, we will not be able to walk in the spirit. As mentioned earlier in the chapter on forgiveness, this requires us dying to self daily so that Christ can dwell within us. Throughout the scripture, we recognize that God's children were rewarded for their obedience.

A BIBLICAL WOMAN OF OBEDIENCE

Now, let's focus on Mary, the beloved mother of Jesus. Luke 1, starting with verse 26 expounds on the story. Mary is a woman who has been revered all over the world, so much so that many parents even named their daughters "Mary" or variations of the name Mary. Mary is also a fine example of a woman who demonstrated obedience to the voice of the Lord. Her obedience led to our Savior Jesus Christ being born and fulfilling His earthly mission. The humble poor virgin woman was born in a small city of Galilee named Nazareth.

One day, Mary received a visit from the angel Gabriel who shared with her that she was highly favored and the Lord was with her. Mary was troubled, but the angel Gabriel reassured her that she had no reason to fear because she has found favor with God and she has been chosen to conceive a son named JESUS who will be the Son of the Most High and He shall be great. As any woman would have, Mary questioned how could this be since she has not been with a man? Gabriel explained to Mary that the Holy Ghost will come upon her and the power of the highest shall overshadow her and the holy thing, which shall be born of her, shall be called the Son of God. Let's imagine how this went down. First, Mary, this virgin woman, receives a visit that she is going to birth a son even though she is still a virgin and then she has to share this with her future husband Joseph and get him to buy into this absurd idea in addition to experiencing the ridicule and shame that comes with a mother who has a child out of wedlock. Then Mary was going to be the mother of the Son of God. Wow! Would you believe this was true? Nonetheless, Mary was obedient to the voice of the Lord shared by the angel Gabriel. She humbly embraced the honor and not only did she birth a son named Jesus, but she also taught her son Jesus to be obedient for thirty years until it was time for Him to fulfill His life mission. Mary watched in agony as her son Jesus died a brutal death on the cross. But the story has a great ending. Jesus resurrected in three days, and Mary could rejoice that her prayers were answered and she was able to witness her son rise from the dead. He is risen!

MODERN DAY WOMAN OF OBEDIENCE

I want to share an experience that changed my life. Several years ago, I use to sell real estate, and suddenly the real estate market crashed, and it became extremely difficult to make sales. I knew it was time to go back to school. Where would I go? How could I stop my life since I was so involved in church as Women's Ministries Leader and had various other commitments? Everyone knew my passion for helping women, children, and families. Unfortunately, I was concerned with their healing so much that it was at the expense of my own health. I eventually burned out and knew it was time for more skills. So, after I received confirmation from three unrelated sources, I knew it was time to go to Loma Linda University in California.

Since I was living in Silver Spring Maryland at the time, this meant I would have to pack up my belongings and move cross-country. I wish I could tell you it was easy once the Lord shared this revelation with me, but I kept walking by sight and not by faith before I decided to be obedient and listen to the voice of the Lord. When I initially applied to the Marriage and Family Therapy Master's Programs at Loma Linda University, the program was full, and they were no longer accepting applicants until the next Fall. I went to one of my dear seasoned prayer warriors at the time, who now rests in peace. I explained my situation to her. After telling her the program was not accepting anyone else, she asked me if I got confirmation from the Lord that I should go. I had to be honest and say yes (since I received three confirmations), she said well then, let us pray over it and ask God to give you the strength to be obedient and start packing for your departure. Being the logical person that I am, I said to myself, if the program is no longer accepting applicants, I do not see the reason to waste my time packing. Nonetheless, she was right; I received a call within a month that someone would not be attending and a spot had opened up. They contacted me, interviewed me, and I was accepted into the program. Everything moved very quickly. I had less than one month to pack up all of my belongings and move cross-country. My mom was concerned about all of my things and worried about the timeline being so short (thanks to my delay) since I own a condo in Maryland. At this point, I wished I would have been obedient to the voice of the Lord when I initially received confirmation. So this time, I was not going to let any other voice deter me from being obedient to the Lord, not even my own.

I finally decided to walk by faith and no longer walk by sight. Let's just say I learned my lesson. Needless to say, I sold all of my furniture within ten days on Craigslist. I had no idea how much help I would still need on the day of my move. The few belongings I had remaining after continuing to pack, I realized it was way more than I initially thought. But God already knew I would underestimate the task of packing and moving across the country. The Holy Spirit impressed the heart of several women from my church including my sister to come to my home the morning of my move to help me finish packing. By God's grace, all of my belongings were either packed, stored at someone's home or the ladies who came to my home that morning took many of my fashionable clothing, paintings or household belongings and rejoiced! As I rushed to the airport thinking that I may not have made my flight, it was as if God cleared out the airport just for me. I walked right in, and there were no lines to rush through. I walked straight through the metal detectors and made it on the plane on time hassle-free. Now, we must admit this is an unusual experience for any airport. Did I fail to mention that when I finally landed in California, an old friend of my cousin (the cousin that I just discovered a few months prior who happened to be one of my three confirmations to attend Loma Linda University) who I never met before came to pick me up at the airport in California and let me stay at her studio apartment rent free for a whole month until I found a place? I am still grateful for her kindness even until this day. This experience helped me to realize that when we are obedient to the Lord, we experience the blessings of the Lord in ways we could never expect. Seven years later, I have completed my Masters and Ph.D. at Loma Linda University in Marital and Family Therapy now known as Couples, Families and Systems and I have already helped hundreds of families in therapy and through speaking engagements at different churches. This is just the beginning. When we are obedient to the voice of the Lord, not only do we experience the blessings of God, but we have no idea who else God will use us to bless. This is why we should never let disobedience cause us to miss our divine appointments with the Lord. How many people will miss out on receiving a blessing that God planned on using us for if we are not obedient to the voice of the Lord?

HOW DO I BECOME A WOMAN OF OBEDIENCE?

While being a woman of obedience can be perceived as something easy to do because God has given us the blueprints on how to live a Christian life, there is one thing that gets in the way every time, and that is, we still need to make a choice every day to follow Jesus. The world is full of temptation to win us over to the wrong side, and if we are not careful, we will give in to sinful flesh. To become a woman of obedience, you need to have a committed relationship with the Lord. It is not enough to depend on your own strength because you will fall short every time. When you spend time with the Lord and study His word, you will learn the things that make Him happy, sad and even angry. It is no different from any other relationship that you have been in. The more you spend time with the person, the better you understand them.

Another important decision that you want to make is the people that you choose to hang around. If you are with people who do not live their lives walking in the fear of the Lord, eventually, you will start to question your own obedience to the Lord and no longer see the importance of being different or you may even feel like it is too awkward to be holy. If you surround yourself with people who love the Lord like you do and everyone wants to be obedient to the Lord, you will have the necessary support that you need to stay on the right track. At the end, we all have to make an individual decision and work out our own salvation. However, it is much easier when you are around like-minds who can even be considered your accountability partners to hold you accountable when you are going down the wrong path. Lastly, pray and fast and ask the Holy Spirit to intercede to help you in areas that are your weak spots. We all have them. God doesn't want us to fail, that is why Jesus left us with the comforter—the Holy Spirit so that we can do greater things than Jesus did when He was on Earth.

MY PRAYER CHALLENGE

Father, today, I ask you to fill my heart with the same measure of love for you that you have for me—sacrificial, unconditional love. The word of God says, "If you love me you will keep my commandments (John 14:15)." Holy Spirit, help me to love God so that I can be obedient to His word in every possible way. Lord, I need your strength and divine intervention to resist the devil in every temptation, and he will flee from me. My desire is to be obedient to the voice of the Lord. Today, I declare that I am a woman of obedience in Jesus' Name. Amen.

ACTION PLAN:
WHAT IS YOUR NEXT STEP AS A WOMAN OF OBEDIENCE?

Lord, my desire is to_____

_____

_____

_____

_____

_____

_____

Lord, today, I make a commitment to _____
_____with the help of
the Holy Spirit.

Lord to grow in my obedience, I will _____

_____

_____

_____

_____

_____

_____

QUALITY #9
A WOMAN OF FAVOR

So shall thou find favor and good understanding in the sight of God and man (Proverbs 3:4, KJV).

Why is it that we find it so hard to believe that God's favor covers our lives? His favor was not just for the children of Israel, but for ALL of His children. Does that mean that you will get everything that you want or live free from trials or tribulations? NO, but what it does mean is that you should expect to experience the power of God in your life in ways that words cannot explain. A woman connected to the Divine Source will have faith and believe that if she asks for something of the Lord and it is according to His will, the Lord will show up and His favor shall be hers. Not because she deserves it, but because she is a child of the King.

A BIBLICAL WOMAN OF FAVOR

A great example of a woman who experienced God's favor and the favor of man is displayed in the Book of Esther. In this story, the king favored Esther, a humble Jewish woman, after Queen Vashti lost her royal estate because of her refusal to obey the command of the drunk King Ahasuerus. Of all the beautiful women the king could have selected, he chose Esther. Esther did not come from an affluent family; both her parents were deceased, and she was raised by her cousin, Mordecai. She was also of Jewish origin, which was not favored in those times. When Esther went before the king, she obtained grace and favor in his sight. Now, Esther was a woman of prayer. When a crisis threatened to annihilate the entire Jewish community, Esther not only told Mordecai to pray and fast for three days as she would but also advised him to have all of her people do the same. She received the king's favor and through her influence over the king, her Cousin—Mordecai, was honored for his faithfulness instead of being put to death, and the Jewish people were saved from extermination. They were able to overcome because God's favor rested with Queen Esther and this, in turn, led to the king's favor resting with her as well. What a remarkable example of God's favor!

A MODERN DAY WOMAN OF FAVOR

I remember earlier on in my professional career when I decided to leave elementary school teaching after five years to pursue a career in management at a nonprofit organization. I was impressed that I wanted to train others and help implement many of the things that I learned as a teacher and in my graduate degree in education. I remember praying and fasting because we were approaching the end of the summer and I started to get nervous because jobs were becoming scarce in the school system. If I ever needed God's favor, this was the time.

So, I applied for an adult day coordinator position because I wanted to be in management and I was getting a bit desperate. I also felt that my teaching background would be able to help me to coordinate activities for the adults and understand them developmentally since often, they had various learning challenges, which caused them to be delayed. Most of them were developmentally on an elementary school level. I remember meeting with the program director who appeared to really like me. While interviewing with her, she looked at my credentials and advised me that I was overqualified for the position that I was applying for and she asked me, "Are you sure you don't want to teach again because that is another option?" I respectfully declined and said I was looking for something more managerial. Fear started to kick in because I had quit my job in faith and the school year had already begun which meant that it would be challenging to get a position in the classroom again. So, after a few moments of silence, she blurted out now that I think about it we are opening up a new position for a compliance specialist and you may be a good fit for it. While we don't have the full job description for it yet, she said maybe we can make it a managerial position. We need someone to keep our three school sites in compliance with state regulations. I had no idea what the state regulations were at the time. When the director asked me, "Are you familiar with the state regulations?" I had to honestly answer no, but the good thing is, I am a quick learner, and I can teach almost anything if given the opportunity. I had a specific salary that I asked God for and would you believe that the director asked me what salary do you want? After I answered, she asked, are you sure? I chimed in yes, and she said she would see what we can do. Unbelievable! It gets better. The director looked at me and said, "I like you" and shortly after that; she informed me that I would be hearing from her soon. She then called another faculty member in the office to walk me back over to human resources. This other faculty member stated that she knows the director well and it is obvious that the Director really likes me, so welcome on board. All I could do was smile.

A few weeks later, I received a call from Human Resources who advised me that I was hired and my starting pay would be what I had asked the Director for, but since the staff was going to receive a raise, my salary would increase. Unbelievable. Not only did I land a job that was exactly what

I asked God for in prayer and fasting, but the truth is that even though I was not qualified for the position, I still ended up with a salary higher than I requested. Is that God's favor or what? Isn't God amazing?

Ladies, if we truly trust in God, we should boldly walk in His favor, expecting God to give us His best. We can be sure that if we believe it, we can receive it. Quite often, we waver in our faith and settle for less because we don't believe that God can do the impossible. So we never get a chance to experience God's best for our lives. I want to challenge you today to believe that you are blessed and highly favored. Expect the best, and you will not be disappointed.

HOW DO I BECOME A WOMAN OF FAVOR?

A woman of favor is a woman who is confident in the Lord. This woman understands that God's favor is for a lifetime (Psalm 30:5). Favor is not for a select group of people, favor belongs to all of us, but we must first believe. God wants to give us exceedingly abundantly above all that we can ask or think but the problem is many of us are shallow thinkers. We expect very little, and we get it every time. If you want to become a woman of favor, there are three things you need to start doing—first speak it, expect it and claim it. Once you have a mindset that you are already walking in God's favor in every area of your life, you will start to experience different outcomes in your life. Stop speaking negativity over your life. You should no longer be entertaining thoughts of defeat, and you need to speak God's favor over your life in spite of the circumstances. Remember, we walk by faith, not by sight. Next, when you expect it, you are no longer worrying about what happens for other people and what is not happening for you because you are always walking in a spirit of expectancy. Lastly, claim it. You should be memorizing all of the scriptures dealing with favor and claiming it daily. The word tells us that he who finds wisdom finds life and shall obtain favor from the Lord (Proverbs 8:35). Ladies, becoming a woman of favor really is a mindset of learning how to have confidence in what the Lord can do for you. First, you must believe that you are a woman of favor.

MY PRAYER CHALLENGE

Lord, when I seek you, I will find you when I search for you with all of my heart (Jeremiah 29:13). Father, help me to pray in faith and believe that I will receive your favor in every situation. I know if I ask according to your will, I shall have it. Today, I declare that I am a woman of favor in Jesus' Name, Amen.

ACTION PLAN:
WHAT IS YOUR NEXT STEP AS A WOMAN OF FAVOR?

Lord, my desire is to_____

_____

_____

_____

_____

_____

_____

Lord, today, I make a commitment to _____

_____with the help of

the Holy Spirit.

Lord to increase favor, I will_____

_____

_____

_____

_____

_____

_____

QUALITY #10

A WOMAN OF SERVICE

But take diligent heed to do the commandment and the law, which Moses the servant of the Lord charged you, to love the Lord your God, and to walk in all his ways, and to keep his commandments, and to cleave unto him, and to serve him with all your heart and with all your soul (Joshua 22:5, KJV).

The best gift you can give is service. Not only will you bless others through your service, but you will also receive an immeasurable blessing. Whether it is going to visit the sick or elderly or lending a listening ear to someone who is experiencing a difficult time in his or her life, the Lord wants us all to become more service-minded and less self-serving. Once we focus on the needs of others, we lose more of ourselves to serve. The Lord tells us to die to self-daily (1 Corinthians 15:31). There is no room for selfishness in the kingdom. Our Creator set the best example of selflessness by sending His only Son, Jesus Christ, who lived on earth, served humanity, taught, healed, and mingled with the people without judging them. You never heard Jesus saying, "What's in it for me?" or "What about me?" He was a humble servant; He always prioritized people and was a caring, loving man. Your actions speak louder than your words about your character. When you walk uprightly, even your enemies are at peace with you. When you focus on others, it relieves you from the stress and burdens of your own life. It also helps you to realize how small your problems really are in the big scheme of things. You can learn to be more grateful for the blessings that God has poured out over your life and start living a Christ-like life.

A BIBLICAL WOMAN OF SERVICE

The biblical story of Ruth reveals a woman who dedicated her life to humble service. Here was a young lady who was now widowed, but instead of focusing on herself and choosing to remarry or return to her homeland, she focused on her mother-in-law. This is an example of true humility. Ruth, who was no longer indebted to her mother-in-law Naomi, refused to abandon her, even after Naomi gave both of her widowed daughters-in-law permission to leave. Ruth chose to sacrifice her life and remain with her mother-in-law to take care of her. Ruth was so abundantly blessed for her service that she did not have room enough to receive it. She was favored every time she went into the fields belonging to Boaz, a man who was kin to her deceased husband. Boaz ordered the reapers to leave extra food for Ruth and instructed them to refrain from treating her like a beggar. Her blessing did not stop there. Naomi told her how to offer herself for marriage to Boaz, instructing Ruth to lie at the foot of his bed when he lay down to sleep. This was the Hebrew custom, and there was no way that Ruth would know this without being told. Boaz sent Ruth back with six measures of barley for her mother-in-law, which was the traditional way of saying yes, I will marry your daughter-in law. Ruth was now going to marry a kind, wealthy, and God-fearing man, all because of her faithful service to her mother-in-law.

The Lord is watching His children, and He will reward you for taking care of your brethren. Don't ever think that a sacrifice you make goes unnoticed by your Heavenly Father, even if your brethren have abused you or have taken you for granted. If our Father counts the hairs on our heads, He is certainly aware of every kind deed we have done to bless others.

A MODERN DAY WOMAN OF SERVICE

I was blessed and fortunate enough to partake in a mission trip to India to assist in conducting health and wellness clinics, do health seminars at schools and provide free screenings. This was a memorable trip for many reasons, but one of the experiences that I remember most was spending a full day in the slums of Mumbai, India. We conducted a health clinic and received word that people walked up to four hours to be seen by the doctor, nurses and support staff on our team. We also had the opportunity to meet one of the pastors who lived close by. What we did not realize was that this pastor was so impressed to help an impoverished community that he and his family decided to pack up their belongings and move in the heart of the slums to serve the community. He recognized that the need was great and he could not develop meaningful relationships and gain the trust of the community if he lived far away. The conditions that many of the members of the community lived in would not have been habitable for many of us because we have been so fortunate. We are afforded so many luxuries that we take for granted on a day-to-day basis. What the pastor chose to focus on most was not his comfort but the fact that there was a need in this community much bigger than him and he felt that he was chosen by God to be used as a vessel to serve a community in dire need.

After we had finished the health clinic, our team went to the Pastor's home to visit, and we met his wife who was a lovely God-fearing woman. I couldn't help but ask myself at the time how did this woman convince herself to pack up and leave her comfort to live in a tiny living quarter that upon entering, you were almost exiting (it was that small)? There was trash everywhere, rodents on the streets, and animals that fed off the trash. There was a stench odor that made many of

87

our stomachs curl. I am not trying to gross you out, but I am just being very honest about what the conditions were and why I could not get this family out of my mind even after we returned to America from India. Many of the neighbors did not have lavatories so they would use the bathroom outdoors. Now, can you understand why I had a challenging time understanding how this woman convinced herself that she would be doing the right thing to pack up her belongings and live under these ghastly conditions with her husband?

When this God-fearing woman came to the door to greet us, she had the brightest and most radiant smile. While we utilized translators, because most of the people on our team did not speak the native language, our team leader offered a word of prayer for the pastor and their family. It was not until I returned to the U.S. and thought of this family and their sacrifice time and time again did I understand how this woman could pack up and leave her life of comfort to serve. This wife was a true woman of God. She was obedient first to God, then to her husband. She was selfless because a selfish woman would not have made this kind of commitment. She was a woman of faith and a woman of prayer. She had to have a relationship with God and spoke with God believing that He would supply all of her needs. She felt that her husband was called by God to serve and as his wife, she too felt called to serve. She did not have to tell her husband to move there without her because she set out on this journey with him and she was probably able to minister to the women in the area as well. What an admirable act of service.

ARE YOU WILLING TO BECOME SELFLESS?

My question to you ladies is: Can you see yourself giving up your comfort if God asked you to go and serve in a

very poor country where you would have to sacr
the amenities and luxuries that you have on a day
Would you go willingly or would you wrestle wi
start negotiating such as the rich young ruler did? He
of the great things that he did for God, but the only
he was not willing to give up was his material wealth. I am not
saying that this is an easy thing to do, so believe me, I am not
just posing this question to you, I am asking myself as well. It
is much easier to talk about the rich young ruler and say I can't
believe how selfish or greedy he was, but the truth is, there is
selfishness in all of us if we could just be honest with
ourselves. Would we be able to sacrifice everything to win
souls for the kingdom? My purpose in sharing this story is to
reflect on the beauty and noble character of this wife. Her
husband must walk around praising her. God may not call each
of us to drastic measures such as moving to the slums of India,
but let's all pray to have servant's hearts and humbly serve in
whatever capacity that God is calling us to serve in.

HOW DO I BECOME A WOMAN OF SERVICE?

Becoming a woman of service is one of the more practical disciplines to develop. Ruth and the pastor's wife in India mentioned above in addition to the life of Jesus does a phenomenal job in displaying what serving from a selfless heart looks like. Now that we also know that studies have demonstrated to us that serving others is one great way of feeling good about yourself, boosting your immune system and promoting well-being, should this not be a practice that we all must embrace? In simple terms, this means at times, saying no to self to say yes to others. It may be second nature to serve in certain capacities like a mother helping her children, but at other times, it may be a sacrifice. Nonetheless, the more you serve, the more you will develop a heart for service.

For example, I enjoy going to hospitals to visit the sick and shut-in whether they are children or adults. It gives me great joy to sing songs of praise and play the guitar for them or simply just spend time with them and pray for them. Going to a nursing home to visit the elderly is another way to serve. Many of the seniors are lonely because several of them do not have any local family, and receive few visits. This is easy when a person has lots of energy and time and may have a desire to do it, but what about on other occasions when you may be tired, and it would be an extra push to bless someone else when they ask for a favor or want you to take them to the supermarket, do their hair or just clean up their homes for them. In the past, someone may ask me to call or visit someone and pray for them, and I may be busy and need to stop what I am doing for the sake of serving someone else. Other times, someone may need a ride home, or financial support and that may require a sacrifice on your part.

One simple way to do this regularly is to schedule it. If you commit yourself to a regular appointment with yourself as you would with everything else in your life, you will be more likely to honor it. Another approach is to join a volunteer community organization that serves in a specific way. If there is a service option in your heart and no one else is doing it, maybe you can put a small group together and start doing it.

Others may be able to choose one service opportunity weekly at a local church. Parents, you may want to volunteer at your child's school to help a teacher and staff at school with few support staff or even volunteer to tutor high-risk children or serve at a soup kitchen. The opportunities are endless. The key is to just serve in one form or another regularly and to bless someone else and in return be immensely rewarded.

MY PRAYER CHALLENGE

Dear Heavenly Father, my prayer is that I would develop a servant attitude just as Ruth and Christ demonstrated in their earthly ministries. Lord, I know that I am naturally self-serving, but I pray that you would change my heart so that my character can become selfless. My desire is to have a heart of love and compassion for others. Lord, help me to enjoy the act of giving more than receiving. Father, God give me a spirit of discernment to discern the needs of those around me so that I can be a blessing to others in whatever way possible. Today, I declare that I am a woman of service in Jesus' Name, Amen.

ACTION PLAN:
WHAT IS YOUR NEXT STEP AS A WOMAN OF SERVICE?

Lord, my desire is to_____

_____

_____

_____

_____

_____

_____

Lord, today, I make a commitment to _____

_____with the help of

the Holy Spirit.

Lord to grow in my service, I will_____

_____

_____

_____

_____

_____

_____

93

QUALITY #11
A WOMAN OF PURPOSE

T o everything there is a season, and a time to every purpose under the heaven (Ecclesiastes 3:1, KJV).

A woman connected to the Divine Source understands that she belongs to her Lord and Savior. She knows that her Heavenly Father has entrusted her to take good care of his TIME, TEMPLE, and TREASURES. Remember, we were bought with a price when Jesus died on the cross and paid for our sins (1 Corinthians 6:20). God doesn't want just a part of us; He wants all of us. To remove our selfish humanistic ways to achieve this, we need help and guidance from the Holy Spirit. Truthfully, this requires something that many women struggle with, DISCIPLINE.

First, let's begin with TIME. When a woman doesn't allocate her time efficiently, it seems as though the days are just passing her by. She is always trying to get something done but never quite completing anything. She goes around in circles, always blaming it on the days, and how they just end too quickly. A woman connected to the Divine Source has a keen sense of time; she doesn't waste it. She recognizes that she must be realistic with her time because it belongs to her Heavenly Father. Her day is organized from early in the morning or the night before, and she makes provisions for unforeseen emergencies. She has a list of things to do each day and sets a realistic time frame for each one of them, so that at the end of the day (although there may still be other things left undone), she is satisfied that her time was spent productively. The Lord will hold us accountable for the use of our time. He expects us to do remarkable things with our time since He has given us all the knowledge and wisdom in addition to access to Him around the clock to seek His counsel and to manage our time in the best way possible. Once we can effectively manage our time, we will be able to maximize the talents that the Lord has blessed us with to fulfill our purpose while we are here.

Next, let's talk about the TEMPLE of the Lord—our bodies. Our temple is not only physical, but it also helps us to connect to God in a spiritual way. A woman must truly understand that her body is the temple of the Lord, to be cherished and maintained (1 Corinthians 6:19). She should always take loving care of herself. Which means she will recognize the importance of exercising regularly, and she will avoid overeating or indulging in foods or drinks that are detrimental to her health. A lot of discipline is required for caring for our temples, and if we are honest with ourselves, we'll admit that we could all use some improvement in this area. Eating worldly foods has changed our taste buds so that we often enjoy foods that are not pleasing in God's sight.

Our diet is important for so many reasons. Many people fail to realize that the ability to overcome sin all begins with appetite. If you reflect on the story of Adam and Eve, it was their failure to control their appetite that caused the first sin to occur. Jesus, on the other hand, defeated the enemy in the wilderness by abstaining from food for 40 days and nights while He fasted and prayed for God's presence and power in His life. Daniel and the three Hebrew boys also refused to partake of the large feast and drink all the wines that the king offered them so that they could maintain clarity of thought and good judgment. Esther asked Mordecai and everyone in the province to pray and fast for three days. Are you beginning to see the pattern? When important life-changing decisions were made, the similarity was that every wise person decided to focus on spiritual food instead of physical food to clearly hear a word from the Lord. It is not by chance that there are fast food restaurants all around us that serve unhealthy meals, which cloud our minds and decision-making skills. The more unclear your mind is, the easier it is to crowd out the voice of the Lord and make poor sinful decisions.

TREASURE

Our Father owns the cattle on a thousand hills. Every good and perfect gift comes from above (James 1:17), but yet, we still feel as though we have the right to pay ourselves first and pay tithes and offerings last or at random. We are not doing the Lord a favor by giving Him what rightly belongs to Him; He doesn't need our money—He just wants to test our hearts and see how faithful we will be to Him when given a choice. "Will a man rob God? Yet he has robbed me in tithes and in offerings. Ye are cursed with a curse for ye have robbed me, even this whole nation. Bring ye all the tithes into the storehouse that there may be meat in mine house, and prove me now herewith, said the Lord of hosts. I will open you the windows of heaven and pour you out a blessing that there shall not be room enough to receive it (Malachi 3:8-10)."

HOW DO I BECOME A WOMAN OF PURPOSE?

Every morning that you wake up, you need to seek God in prayer to ask Him: "What is my assignment for today?" When you know your purpose, it makes life more meaningful and worth living. A woman should never enter the day oblivious to what her plan is for the day. From the night before or the morning after, every woman should have her day planned out with the understanding that if God has a special assignment for that day, it will take precedence over any plan or list of things that needs to be done for that day. A woman with purpose knows that her time, temple and treasure belongs to the Lord, so she seeks God daily to make sure that she is walking with the Lord and fulfilling her purpose. A woman of purpose knows the importance of her temple, and she does not just put anything in her body. She eats temperately with purpose, recognizing that what she eats can obstruct her mind and if her mind is not clear, she will not be able to hear the voice of the Lord and fulfill her assignment for the day. A woman of purpose recognizes that she is a steward of what God has loaned her and God requires a tenth of all that she has, so she is disciplined and diligent with her money and does not spend capriciously. We must be good stewards of our time, temple, and treasures and believe that God knows the plans He has for us—plans to prosper us, and give us hope of a good future (Jeremiah 29:11).

A few tips to becoming a woman of purpose is to first take ownership of each day. No longer walk into each day wondering what happened to the day, your time, or your plans but seek God's wisdom upon rising and before going to bed each night to make sure that you are not just planning a list but you are walking in your purpose. Next, find purpose driven women to spend your time with. When you are around other women who are purpose driven, you will have accountability and be more eager to stay focused and fulfill that plan that God has for you. Lastly, as always, stay in prayer and in the word. When you seek God, you will find Him when you search for Him with all your heart. Set aside times for prayer and quiet time with the Lord for you to hear His voice and determine how He is leading you. Remember, you want to be led by God, not the other way around. God is perfect in His wisdom, and His infinite power can help us to see things that we will miss with our restricted vision. Let God lead and be willing to follow. God can help you to understand how the past, present, and future will all fit together and help you to make a master plan to bring each assignment to completion. Remember ladies, God's way is always the best way.

MY PRAYER CHALLENGE

Dear Heavenly Father, my desire is to become a woman of purpose. Lord, help me to use my time, temple, and treasures for the glory of God. Lord, I want to live a purpose driven life and be an example to the secular and Christian world. Help me to fulfill my daily assignments and the divine appointments you set before me each day. Father, I pray that you would order my steps and I would be obedient, self-disciplined and a doer of your word. Father, God, today, I declare that I am a woman of purpose in Jesus' Name, Amen.

ACTION PLAN:
WHAT IS YOUR NEXT STEP AS A WOMAN OF PURPOSE?

Lord, my desire is to_____

_____

_____

_____

_____

_____

_____

Lord, today, I make a commitment to _____

_____with the help of

the Holy Spirit.

Lord to grow as a woman of purpose, I will_____

_____

_____

_____

_____

_____

_____

QUALITY #12
A WOMAN OF GRACE

L et no corrupt communication proceed out of your mouth, but that, which is good to the use of edifying, that it may minister grace unto the hearers (Ephesians 4:29, KJV).

A true woman of God recognizes the power of her tongue. The power to build her house or tear it down. She prays to keep her tongue from all evil (Psalm 34:13 KJV). For she knows it is as sharp as a sword (Psalm 57:14, KJV).

The saying goes, "sticks and stones may break my bones but words will never hurt me." If this is not false, I don't know what is. You might forget about physical pain after the wounds heal, but you may be permanently scarred by unkind words. It tears a little part of you each time someone speaks evil over your life. It's been said that 12 positive statements are needed to replace one negative statement. That says a lot about the impact that the tongue has over our lives. We must learn to think positive thoughts and let these be reflected in our words. I am fearfully and wonderfully made (Psalm 139:14). I can do all things through Christ who strengthens me (Philippians 4:13). I will bless the Lord at all times. His praise shall continually be in my mouth (Psalms 34:1). Speak words of life over your children, siblings, husband, friends, and family, and watch how they start to grow. Others will also enjoy being in your presence more. You will not only become more favored and a joy to be around, but you will also start a chain reaction. As you begin to build others up, it becomes contagious, and others will, in turn, build you up too! It goes on and on. The world will become a better place; people will experience more success than failure just by believing in themselves. We will build nations of positivity and leave a legacy behind for the next generation.

A BIBLICAL WOMAN OF GRACE

In a town named Joppa, there was a certain disciple named Tabitha also known as Dorcas (the first Greek name of a female in the New Testament). The Book of Acts 9:32-43 gives a short synopsis of the life of this graceful woman. We do not know much about the family and genealogy of Dorcas, but what we do know is that she was a Christian. This holy woman of God was admired by the community and esteemed by all for her good works and service to humanity. Then suddenly, Dorcas becomes ill and dies. Her body is washed and cared for and then laid out in an upper room. This was a sad day of mourning. All of the widows wept and shared the coats and garments that Dorcas made for them while she was with them. Dorcas was a model to the church and the community. She was a woman with a servant heart who spent her life caring for those in need.

Her fellow disciples at church learned that Peter was close by and two members went to the apostle, requesting that he visits the grieving community of believers. They were aware of Peter's supernatural power, and they all had faith and believed that Dorcas would live again. The Bible says that Peter knelt, prayed and turned to the body of Tabitha and said, "Arise," and she opened her eyes and when she saw Peter, she sat up. This miraculous scene caused many to believe in the Lord. One question that I would like to ask is why did God allow this woman to be raised from the dead? I would like to suggest because her life was such a blessing to all, her miraculous revival would do more to win souls for the kingdom than her death. This story has several great lessons that we can learn and apply to our lives. One is that this great community of faith came together with a common goal in mind, believing that Tabitha's life should be restored. Second, Tabitha's life was such a testimony that the church and community revered her for her good works. Lastly, God answers the prayers of those who join their faith together for a worthwhile cause even it seems impossible from a human perspective. There is nothing too hard for God to do, even using Peter to pray for Tabitha to be raised from the dead for the glory of God! And Tabitha rose! Hallelujah!

A MODERN DAY WOMAN OF GRACE

Many Presidents' wives demonstrate poise, elegance, and gracefulness. Their husbands have some of the most powerful positions in the world, and they are watched globally. They are judged, criticized or praised based on what they do, wear, say or fail to say. We can all agree while this is a revered position to be in, it is by far not an easy one. The woman that I want to focus on in spite of your political view is one that I greatly admire, Michelle Obama. This woman has exemplified grace in many ways. Not only was this woman already powerful and intelligent within her own right as a lawyer who graduated from a top IVY League school, but the way our 44th President Barack Obama praised her as a wife and mother publicly gives you a glimpse into their marriage and family. Michelle's ability to keep her family first and maintain certain rituals and routines in the midst of all of the demands of the White House was admirable. Her service to the community, whether it was her focus on inner city girls, her push for a garden at the White House to promote health and prevent obesity nationwide, her "Let's Move" campaign to promote exercise, her push for girls to receive education around the world who are unable to gain basic access, or her invitations extended to the public to visit the White House; Michelle Obama will be remembered as one of the most caring, intelligent, personable, beautiful inside and out Presidents' wives. In my perspective, this is what I deem to be a modern day woman of grace.

HOW DO I BECOME A WOMAN OF GRACE?

A woman of grace is a woman of integrity who demonstrates elegance in her presence. A graceful woman exhibits maturity even in difficult circumstances. This is a woman who has learned through life experience not to let anything move her or take her off course. This woman understands the power of prayer and recognizes that prayer changes things. To become a woman of grace, you have to be connected to the divine source at all times. Start each day off with praise and thanksgiving and commune with your Heavenly Father in prayer. Study the word of God to be reminded of the life of Christ as well as many of the Godly women displayed in the Bible (many of them are mentioned in this book: Esther, Ruth, Abigail, Mary, the woman with the issue of blood, etc.) As a woman of grace, you should never take for granted that you are an example to others and you know that you have an audience wherever you go, so you are always mindful of what you say and do. People are observing you daily, and it all begins at home. Being a woman of grace means you model kindness, gentleness, patience, forgiveness, empathy, and compassion. You often demonstrate love through your actions; therefore, you are known to be servant-minded. As you read the qualities of a woman connected to the divine source, you can recognize that a woman of grace has many of the characteristics of all of the qualities written about in this book. This woman is noble in stature and upright in all her ways. The trials and tribulations faced in her life have helped her to become stronger. As we grow in Christ, and learn how to trust God with all of our hearts, and thank Him for the trials and tribulations that we face, we will gain countless victories and become women of grace too!

MY PRAYER CHALLENGE

Dear Lord, today, I pray that I will use my tongue to edify, uplift, and bless others so that I may be a better example of Christ. Help me to never wrongfully judge others based on their appearance or lifestyle when I do not know their stories. Lord, forgive me for tearing others down or gossiping in the past and help me to be a graceful Godly woman in my speech and in my actions. Holy Spirit, help me to be a better Christian. Today, I declare that I am a woman of grace in Jesus' Name, Amen.

ACTION PLAN:
WHAT IS YOUR NEXT STEP AS A WOMAN OF GRACE?

Lord, my desire is to_____

_____

_____

_____

_____

_____

_____

Lord, today, I make a commitment to _____

_____with the help of

the Holy Spirit.

Lord to grow in grace, I will_____

_____

_____

_____

_____

_____

_____

EPILOGUE
A WOMAN OF VIRTUE

Who can find a virtuous woman? For her price is far above rubies (Proverbs 31:10, KJV).

Have you ever thought about why the Proverbs 31 woman always receives praise? Have you ever taken the time to read and meditate on the character of this woman? Let's start from the beginning. Virtue is defined as moral excellence; righteousness. So, here is a woman who builds her house. It doesn't matter if a woman is single, married, or just growing into womanhood; what matters is that she realizes her place as a woman. The Proverbs 31 woman is rare, not your everyday woman. This is a woman to be admired. I learn something new each time I study Proverbs 31:10-31. God wants to take us to a new level. He is encouraging us to use our time and tongues wisely; to move us away from tearing people down through our gossip, complaints, and negativity. He doesn't want us to cause destruction in anyone; He desires to purify us. God wants us to be holy. He is helping us to rise above the ordinary and become extraordinary women in the Lord. In essence, the Lord wants His daughters to be caring, compassionate, empathetic, strong, wise, and trustworthy. He wants us to be women with standards of excellence.

I went to a funeral once and was amazed at what I witnessed. I saw a woman over the age of 80 who was just as beautiful as could be, lying peacefully in her casket, as if she was just taking a nap. When her biography was read, and her family and childhood friends spoke about her, the first thing that came to my mind was how much she sounded like the Proverbs 31 woman. She was a woman of service; one who was kind, giving, caring, and filled with love. She rose early in the morning to feed her children and grandchildren, worked in the field where she planted her crops and took good care of her husband. This patient woman always had a kind word on her tongue. This was indeed a woman to be praised. Thinking of how she took care of everyone else, you would have thought she would have looked really haggard and worn, but instead, she looked 20 years younger. She was more beautiful than ever as she gracefully rested in her casket.

OUR PRAYER CHALLENGE

Lord, our prayer is to become selfless in all that we do. Grant us compassion that we may have Christ-like characters. We desire to be more kind, caring, and loving. Please help us to become women who build their homes, not tear them down. Whether we are single, married, mothers, or widows, Lord, please show us the way.

A WOMAN OF VIRTUE

- Today, we celebrate you for being a woman of virtue!
- A woman who demonstrates the love of God in everything she does
- A woman who displays humility, compassion and integrity in the way she loves
- A woman who does not brag or boast and is accepting of most
- A woman who embraces God's children and makes them feel included in all that she does
- A woman without many words but even in her silent cues
- You can see that she is a woman of virtue
- When you are in her presence you feel welcomed by her smile, kind deeds or gestures
- At other times she may just ask where have you been?
- And in that moment, you know her heart is true and that she really cares about you
- A woman that doesn't take credit because she understands that she is a woman of service
- And in the end, God will say well done my good and faithful servant!
- A woman who cares for all people despite their flaws
- And empathizes with you no matter who you are
- A woman that is always positive even in the midst of her bad days
- A woman who loves God and lives her life His way
- A woman who knows her strength comes from a higher source that is not her own
- A woman of excellence who cares and knows the importance of keeping God near
- In spite of what people say or do, you are a woman of core values

- You are a fine example of a woman of God that lives a Christian life
- Your husband is indeed a blessed man to have you as his wife!
- Thank you for being a woman of VIRTUE in all that you do, we really love and admire you!

By Wendy Wray

HOW DO I BECOME A WOMAN OF VIRTUE?

While I believe that all of the biblical and modern day women shared in this book are great examples of how to become a Virtuous Woman, I believe there is no better book in the Bible that can demonstrate the gentleness, grace, and virtue of women than the Proverbs 31 woman. This virtuous woman is my hero. She is a fine example of a woman. The life of this admirable woman says it all. Her life displays love, wisdom, business acumen, a heart for the poor, a heart of service, and kindness on her tongue.

She is a wife who is peaceful, purposeful, compassionate, service-oriented, graceful, obedient, prayerful, faith-filled, patient, a helper to her husband, children, and even the maidens in her gate. This woman is so amazing that she receives the praise and honor of her family. This is indeed a woman worthy of praise. If you don't believe me, read it for yourself. (Proverbs 31:10-31)

Who can find a wife of noble character? She is worth more than the costliest jewels. Her husband has confidence in her abilities. He will never be poor. All her life she will do him good and will never do anything to harm him.

She supplies her house with wool and linen and does her work eagerly. She supplies her home with food brought by ships from all over the world. She rises while it is still dark to lay out the day's food for the family and plan the day's work for her servant girls.

She looks at some land and buys it; with her earnings, she plants a vineyard. She works with energy and puts all her strength into her tasks. She knows the value of what she sells

116

and often works late into the night. She spins her own thread and weaves cloth with her own hands.

She gives generously to the poor and helps those who are in need. She doesn't worry about her family in winter they have double garments for warmth. She makes her own curtains and bedspreads; her clothes are tasteful and beautiful. Her husband is respected because of her and is chosen to sit with the city officials. She markets beautiful clothes and belts, and sells them to merchants. She is respected in her own right and is not afraid of the future. She speaks words of gentle wisdom and teaches kindness to others. She is never lazy and watches over the affairs of her family. Her children respect her and say so, and her husband praises her, saying, "Many women do wonderful things, but you surpass them all." Charm is deceptive and beauty disappears, but a woman who honors the Lord will be praised. Reward her for what she has done. Let her works be praised by everyone in the city.

Ladies, we have come to the end of our journey together. I hope you have prayerfully sought counsel from the Lord on where you may need change or improvement. I am so excited about the changes that you will make with the help of the Holy Spirit. Read this book as many times as you need to until you make the necessary changes. Change does not occur overnight; it is a process. You have read the qualities that will help you to become a Proverbs 31 woman in this modern day. I hope and pray that you will recognize the importance of your life testimony and how it impacts those around you. Remember, even when you don't know it, you always have an audience watching you, and if that isn't enough, know that your Heavenly Father always has His eyes on you. May you become a new creature in Christ as old things pass away and all things become new (2 Corinthians 5:17). May you openly embrace change, become changed and be a great inspiration for all of the women in your life and my hope is that you will help to create generational changes in your family.

My prayer is that every woman reading this book would prayerfully ask the Lord for strength to work on exemplifying these amazing qualities in their lives. Having the desire to be more like the Proverbs 31 woman by itself is VIRTUOUS. To become a woman of virtue, we must all recognize that a woman who fears the Lord shall be praised!